Action Keys for Success

■ ■ ■

Anointed Power

By Prince Handley

University of Excellence Press

1

Copyright © 2009 by Prince Handley
All Rights Reserved.

UNIVERSITY OF EXCELLENCE PRESS
Los Angeles ■ London ■ Tel Aviv

ISBN-13: 978-0692248249
ISBN-10: 0692248242

Printed in the U.S.A.

First Edition

■

The only book you need on Success

TABLE OF CONTENTS

FOREWORD

There is a time to rest, there is a time to heal, there is a time to reflect and **there is a time to regroup**.

This book is NOT modeled after the many other books on success. You can apply the principles in this book and see performance immediately. **The past can be "turned around" and loss can be recovered**.

This is a "street" publication – where the rubber hits the road – dealing with KEYS to success. You will develop a spirit of **excellence** applying these **simple** principles.

This book is for "losers" **who want to become "winners!"** Why do I say "losers?" Because if you're NOT happy where you're at – or NOT satisfied with your achievements – then you're NOT winning.

I'm going to put you on your way. You don't need to buy anything else ... you don't need to stop eating pizza. **You can even enjoy yourself ... and people!**

That BIG DREAM in your gut ... it's ready to fly out! Hold on, you haven't seen anything yet!

View the *Table of Contents* on the previous page and get excited. **The NEW YOU is about to excel greatly!**

4

Action Keys for Success

■ ■ ■

Anointed Power

ACTION

Action is the process of doing something to achieve an aim. Actions speak louder than goals because what one does means more than what one plans. **Goals are good, but without action they are infertile and sterile . . . they are uninspired and uninventive.**

I believe in setting goals, and I have taught the importance of goal setting for 50 years. However, there are times in your life and ministry where you will have to **force yourself** to take – or possibly, maintain – action. That is what this book is about!

I want you to burn the following scriptures into your mind:

- *"Be ye strong therefore, and let not your hands be weak: for your work shall be rewarded."* [2 Chronicles 15:7]

- *"Therefore, my beloved brethren, be ye steadfast, unmovable, always abounding in the work of the Lord, forasmuch as ye know that your labor is not in vain in the Lord."* [1 Corinthians 15:58]

- *"And let us not be weary in well doing: for in due season we shall reap, if we faint not."* [Galatians 6:9]

There is a time to rest, there is a time to heal, there is a time to reflect, there is a time to regroup . . . however, **let God lead you in these times**. Be led of the Spirit in these times just as you are in the days of battle. **Never quit!** We only regroup so that we may advance in battle more powerfully and effectively.

Recently I have been re-studying the life of King David. I felt as though I were with him. I almost cried when reading and reflecting upon the consequences of his sin. It is plain to see where David's problem started:

6

"And it came to pass, after the year was expired, at the time when kings go forth to battle, that David sent Joab, and his servants with him, and all Israel; and they destroyed the children of Ammon, and besieged Rabbah. But David tarried still at Jerusalem." [2 Samuel 11:1]

Lust, adultery, murder, fourfold judgment on his family: these were the results of NOT going to war at the time of year when the other kings went to battle. In this book I am going to help you make sure that NEVER happens in your life.

It is interesting to notice that **things turned around for King David** after HE turned around. In 2 Samuel 18:1-4 we read that, *"David numbered the people that were with him, and set captains of thousands and captains of hundreds over them."* David then split the warriors up into three parts under the leadership of his top three generals, and said to the people, *"I will surely go forth with you myself also."* But the people said to him, *"You shall not go forth (with us) . . . for you are worth ten thousand of us . . . it is better that you aid us from the city."* And David answered, *"What seems best to you I will do."*

Notice that David's **intent** was to go to battle with his army; this is what is important: the intent of the heart. He had learned his lesson the hard way. **Never stop fighting**, at least in the intent of your heart. **You must MAINTAIN a "warrior" mentality**.

You must have spiritual and mental control of the situation at all times. Even in times of "R and R" (rest and recreation) you must maintain a warrior attitude and be **listening to God for instructions** about the future battle(s).

Your job is to constantly appropriate victory through faith as you listen to and obey the voice of the Spirit for the glory of God.

YOU CAN NOT STOP FIGHTING . . . EVER!!!

IF YOU DON'T QUIT ... YOU'LL WIN,
BUT IF YOU QUIT, YOU CAN'T WIN!

This is a message for many of God's workers. Many people either:

- Have not fulfilled their heart's desires in their life's calling (including service for God);
- Are not enjoying their work (including service for God); or,
- Have been (or are being) beaten up by the enemy (and, sometimes by God's children).

Whenever asked about the secret of his success, real estate developer and billionaire, Donald Trump, always answers, *"Do what you enjoy!"*

It's true. **We must be excited about our work ...** especially those people who are serving God.

The purpose of this book is to both CHALLENGE you and HELP you:

- Enjoy your work;
- Do what you want; and,
- Maintain victory so that you can always take action.

Be the person you always wanted to be . . . make it happen!

King Solomon said, *"There is nothing better for a man, than that he should eat and drink, and that he should make his soul [enjoy] good in his labor. This also I saw, that it was from the hand of God."* [Ecclesiastes 2:24]

Many people are "stale" and not on the cutting edge because they do NOT enjoy their work. They love God but are lacking the anointing to be a "new sharp threshing instrument." [Isaiah 41:15] The enemy's job is to get you discouraged . . . and then to lose your vision.

If this describes you, I have some good news for you. If you will do what I teach you in this book, things will begin to change. **Do some fasting, get alone, and seek God.**

Then, in the Spirit, tear down the walls that are limiting you. Take your authority, BELIEVE GOD for the things you once desired! Get back on track.

Don't give up, and don't take LESS than the best! Let me repeat that: **Don't take less than the best!**

- Fast, get alone, seek God;

- Tear down the walls that are limiting you;

- Take your authority;

- Believe God for the things you once desired;

- Get back on track;

- Don't give up; and,

- Don't take less than the best!

Remember, if you don't quit, you'll win ... but if you quit, you can't win!

There was a movie several years ago titled *"Stuck On You"* which starred Matt Damon and Cher. It was about two brothers who were Siamese twins. Finally, the brothers realized they needed to be separated (physically) in order to do what each brother wanted to fulfill in his lifetime. They reached this decision when one brother asked the other, *"What is that thing you want to do MOST in the world?"* And then he challenged his brother with this admonition: *"You have to do it!"*

10

Let me recommend **eight (8) steps to take** in order to help get you out of your "desensitized spirituality" and into the vortex of God's anointing:

[1] As much as possible, stop all activity for a while, even ministry.

[2] Get "loose," relax, and enjoy God.

NOTE: Many times you will be tempted to start a new ministry or outreach right away (while relaxing in your time of rest). That would be like shooting yourself in the foot while you're walking to the hospital. If God has given you NEW ideas or directives, take skeletal notes (or even copious notes if you feel the necessity). Then store the notes for the future time of implementing the project(s). You will find that, as you're relaxing in the sunshine of God's love, an abundance of ideas will come to you.

[3] Take time to dream.

Albert Einstein, perhaps the greatest mathematician and physicist of the last century, had two (2) major assets:

- A childlike questioning character (like a four or five-year-old); and,
- An intellectual capacity to think beyond.

Let me ask you a question: *"How long has it been since you asked your Heavenly Father some childlike questions?"* Questions like:

- What can I do to share God's love with every nation and tribe for Messiah Yeshua?

- What is the KEY thing I can do that will impact nations the most?

- What are new ways to market the Good News?

- What are some secrets of the universe that nobody knows?

- What do you [God] like about me [yourself] the most?

How long has it been since you:

- Discarded all your ideas about how to serve God?

- Researched new trends and new cultural evolutionary movements?

- Asked a lost person how they would reach the world with the message and love of Messiah?

- Studied the ants?

- Studied seeds, climatology, and weather patterns?

[4] Know who you are. Read through the epistles; learn once again WHO you are in Christ and WHAT you have in Christ.

You have to come to the place, once again, where you KNOW the calling and destiny that has been designed for you before the foundation of the world.

True holiness, and also true Biblical prosperity, is to KNOW that **you're working "hand-in-hand" with God** to shake nations for Christ.

[5] Meditate.

Find the scriptures ("rhema" Words) in the Holy Bible that speak to you **concerning your calling and destiny** and **dwell on them**. Speak them to yourself.

See yourself doing the things involved with your calling and destiny. **Image them upon the screen of your mind**. See the places and the activities and then THANK God for their fulfillment. Receive them by faith.

- See
- Speak
- Thank
- Receive

[6] Change your environment (and maybe your friends).

This is why God sent his servants into different areas, sometimes as a result of hard-times. It's a lot easier if you do it for yourself, with the leading of the Holy Spirit.

Imitational faith is the copying of ministry styles used by others; it results in not only lack of creativity, but also "inbreeding" in the Body of Christ.

Be yourself -- be original. **Don't be afraid to be different**. Study the lifestyles of God's servants through the centuries: in the Bible, and throughout Christian church history. Study Prince Handley's book: *Militant Church History*.

[7] Re-evaluate your goals.

Which ones have been accomplished?

Are there any goals that you feel you should scrap for now, or permanently?

Which ones are not accomplished yet? **Ask yourself**:

- Why are they not accomplished?
- Where are you in your time line, or schedule, for their fulfillment?
- What action will you take to implement them in a timely fashion?

Are there any new goals or projects God wants you to undertake?

If so, do they fit into the general scheme of your other goals?

Are they completely separate from your other goals?

[8] Make your plans fit into God's plans.

The GREATEST ADVICE I can give you concerning your plans is as follows:

IF YOUR PLANS FIT INTO GOD'S PLANS . . .

YOU WILL HAVE GOD'S FAITH . . .

AND GOD'S FAITH ALWAYS WORKS!

Cry out to God and tell Him you want to be used greatly by Him ... that you don't want to come home to Heaven until you've fulfilled, with excellence, your calling and your destiny.

And remember the words of King Solomon: *"He that fears God will come forth of them all."*

We are to fear God . . . NOT men, demons, or anything else. The enemy knows if he can get you to fear anyone or anything other than God, he can cancel your fear of God and thereby void the operation of wisdom in your life . . . at least temporarily until you become aware of what's happening.

You have to "shut off" the ideas of fear and replace them with IDEAS OF FAITH. Use visual thoughts when you have thoughts of concern. You will eliminate most of Satan's attacks on your mind. You will also destroy Satanic activity in its tracks!

When you have thoughts of fear, replace them with VISUAL THOUGHTS. So when you have thoughts of fear about your family, your possessions, your health or your ministry, replace them with VISUAL THOUGHTS. See the Holy Angels ministering to, blessing and guarding your family, your possessions, your health, and your ministry.

By visualizing your thoughts, **you can even add emphasis (power and potency) to them by decreeing them**. Use the Holy Angels in your thoughts – see them helping you. **See and declare aloud the BLOOD of Christ over everything that God has given you by birth, adoption or assignment ... both now and in the future.**

If we turn back God cannot fight for us. Why? Because, when we turn our back, we are disobeying our leading and our Leader. We are not taking action.

We will not see real miracles unless we put ourselves in a position in which God can work for us. God works in the area of the impossible. What is impossible with men is possible with God.

You may not need direction.
You may just need to go forward = ACTION.

There is an old saying, *"You are as others see you."* **The devil knows if you have FEAR in your heart**. If you do, **ask God to help you: to take the fear away**. King David said, *"What time I am afraid, I will trust in thee (the LORD)."* [Psalm 56:3] Go to the Word of God and RECEIVE BY FAITH the power promised in the scriptures, such as:

"For God has not given us the spirit of fear; but of power, and of love, and of a sound mind." [2 Timothy 1:7] **Fear is a spirit; therefore, you must speak to it.** God is love and He is spirit. Love is stronger than fear. Perfect love casts out fear.

"There is no fear in love; but perfect love casts out fear: because fear has torment. He that fears is not made perfect in love." [1 John 4:18]

If you are afraid of someone, ask God to give you His love for them.

You can bind fear in the name of Jesus, and cast it away from you. Command it to leave, and use the name of Jesus against it. Speak (declare) the BLOOD of Christ against it.

It is your responsibility to overcome fear. SERIOUS cases of fear require four (4) steps:

- A stayed (fixed) mind.
- Confession of God's Word [1 John 4:18; James 4:7; and 2 Timothy 1:7].
- A step of faith . . . action. Speak to fear and take authority over it.
- Intercession and spiritual warfare (for others or one's self).

IMPORTANT

THE REASON FOR THIS ATTACK OF FEAR IS TO GET YOU TO STOP ACTION

The enemy's chief concern is that you STOP doing what you are currently involved in doing. You have been TOO SUCCESSFUL; also, your plans for future endeavors are causing him to freak out. **The devil is the most frustrated person in the world today; he knows that his time is running out.** When the fullness of the Gentiles takes place, then all Israel (the nation as a whole) will be saved. [Romans 11]

Sun Tzu, in his book, *The Art of War*, says *"Every battle is won before it is fought."* How true in Christian warfare: even **the whole war is won because of the victory of our Lord Messiah Yeshua (Jesus, the Anointed One)**. His death, burial, and resurrection conquered the enemy and bought our freedom and eternal life. Now . . . **we take ACTION on that victory by appropriating it in faith as we move forward.**

Another weapon in the arsenal of the enemy, in addition to fear, is shame. The enemy will try to attack you with imposed shame.

Lots of times, the enemy will attack even seasoned warriors with imposed shame from family members or friends as a result of some "slip up" from the past.

There are many examples of shame experienced by people of God in the Bible. None of us are perfect: that's why we need a Savior! Abraham (the same as) sold his wife two times. Moses killed a man in anger.

David committed adultery and murder. Peter denied Messiah three times in one night.

We see that Adam's shame was manifested in hiding. In Revelation 3:18, Jesus admonished the Church at Laodicea to " ... *buy of me white raiment, that you may be clothed, [so] that the shame of our nakedness does not appear . . .*"

There are several types of shame:

- Adamic shame
- Inherited shame
- Actual shame
- Imposed shame

The verdict of guilt, whether real or imagined, is shame. It may be something **inherited from Adam** (who brought sin into the world as the federal head of the race); or it may be something **inherited from ancestral, or family lines.** It may be **actual shame, resulting from an action you have initiated.** And – it may be **psychological shame – real or false shame** that people or demon spirits have tried to impose upon you, resulting in oppression, rejection, physical or mental sickness, and lack of production.

Every one of these types of shame may be remitted, or canceled, by the **atonement** of Christ. **The BLOOD of Christ paid for you and your sins, and provides healing for shame.**

Jesus Christ bore your shame. Hebrews 12:2 tells us that our Lord Jesus despised the shame of the cross and his nakedness thereon, but went through it because of the JOY set before Him: that is, he saw YOU able to be made whole and to know God, with your sins forgiven and having eternal life, as the result of His sacrifice. Jesus despised shame . . . and He despises it in YOUR life. He died for YOU so that you do NOT have to carry shame. He carried it for YOU!

He is alive to remit guilt and its resultant shame from your life today. You can appropriate the healing in His shed BLOOD for you by calling on Him today. Pray and ask Him to deliver you.

You can get back up . . . because He got back up! The Master has need of you in these last days.

Along with fear and imposed shame, the enemy will also, at times, try to attack the seasoned warrior of Christ with mental oppression. Again, I have some Good News for you.

Oppression – both mental and physical – is included in Christ's work FOR US. Christ was driven; he was abased and looked down upon. Isaiah 53:7 says, *"He was **oppressed** and he was **afflicted** ... "*

- The Hebrew word for **"oppress"** [nagas] in this passage means **"to drive, to harass, to tyrannize, to oppress.**"

- The original Hebrew word used for **"afflicted"** [anah] means **"to look down upon, depress, abase, humble.**"

Christ was driven; he was abased and looked down upon. In Isaiah 53:4, where it reads, *" ... he carried our pains,"* the literal Hebrew meaning is **"acute pain; intense suffering: MENTAL or PHYSICAL.**"

In Psalm 41, a Psalm of David written 1,000 years before Christ, Kind David writes, *"LORD, be merciful unto me: heal my soul, for I have sinned against you."* [Verse 4]

The Hebrew word here used for **"soul"** is **"nephesh"** which refers to not only the mind, but also the heart: **healing for the intellect, the emotion, and the will**, as well as the body. Jesus "carried" sickness, sin, disease, poverty and oppression - the "works" of the devil (Satan) - FOR YOU! Now . . . **YOU don't have to carry them any longer!** They do NOT belong to the believer in Messiah!

Jesus healed the separation between God and man through His work on the cross-stake (the atonement) FOR US, and therefore ended Satan's dominion over ALL who would trust in Christ. *"For this purpose the Son of God was manifested, that He might DESTROY the works of the devil."* [1 John 3:8]

➡ **SECRET #1 - Action, including intercession, is the key thing Satan is afraid of in your life and ministry**. He has to STOP your action. But he can't if you do NOT let him! *"The kingdom of heaven suffers violence, and the violent take it by force."* [Matthew 11:12] The Greek word for "**violent**" here used is "biastes" and means a "forcer" or "**one who is energetic**." The devil is AFRAID of your ENERGY directed towards the kingdom!

FOLLOW THIS MODEL:
EFFORT - ENERGY - ENTHUSIASM

Notice that **most of the attacks Satan makes against you are in the realm of the mind** through lies: telling you that you are ill, weak, going to die . . . or using imposed shame, fear, or discouragement. **This is why you must be proactive**.

DECLARE the BLOOD of Christ over your body, mind, soul and spirit each day. (This way, even your emotions are covered.)

➡ **SECRET #2** - It's interesting to note that one of the names of the devil is "**Beelzebub**." The original Hebrew name means "**Lord of the flies**" and was the name of a Philistine [Palestinian] god. It was a "**dung god**" . . . a "**manure god**." What a wonderful title for Satan: "**Lord of the maggots ... the manure god!**" Dead blood draws flies.

➡ **SECRET #3** - GOOD NEWS! **The BLOOD of Jesus repulses Satan and his demons**. Speak the BLOOD over your home and family. Just as the Israelites applied the BLOOD to their doors so that the death angel would pass over, so you can apply the BLOOD of Christ over your family and home by speaking it in faith over them. [Torah: Exodus Chapter 12]

If you would like to know the Messiah personally, **you can**. Just invite Him into your life NOW by praying this prayer:

"God in Heaven, I know that I have sinned and I want to be forgiven. Please forgive me. I want your Son, Messiah Jesus, to take over my life NOW. I invite Jesus to come into my life and to be my Lord. Please help me to live for you on earth, and take me to Heaven when I die. Amen."

Declare the BLOOD of Christ over your loved ones daily and over all that God has given you by birth, adoption, or assignment!

In case you ever become – or have already been – a victim of any of these attacks of Satan, and have suffered loss of spiritual or physical dominion, I have again some Good News for you. **What has caused you to suffer loss**: Sin? Disobedience? Bad decision? Attack from the enemy?

Whatever it was, God CAN turn the situation around for you. God WANTS to turn it around for you!

There are FOUR (4) major points to consider for recovering your loss:

- Realize there is a turning point - a good future. (Remember King David.)
- Do what God tells you to do. Pray, listen, and obey.
- Make your past glorify God.
- Go forward.

OTHER SCRIPTURES FOR RECOVERING LOSS

"So I will restore to you the years . . . the locust [the enemy] has eaten. You will eat in plenty and be satisfied, and praise the name of the LORD your God, who has dealt wondrously with you; My people will never be put to shame." [Joel 2:25-26]

"As for you also, because of the blood of your covenant, I will set your prisoners free from the waterless pit. Return to the stronghold, you prisoners of hope. Even today, I declare that I will restore DOUBLE to you." [Zechariah 9:11-12]

"Instead of your shame you will have DOUBLE honor, and instead of confusion they will rejoice in their portion. Therefore, in their land they will possess DOUBLE." [Isaiah 61:7]

"I will multiply upon you man and beast; and they will increase and bear young [be fruitful]; I will make you inhabited as in former times, and do better for you than at your beginnings. Then you will know that I am the LORD." [Ezekiel 36:11]

"And the LORD turned the captivity of Job, when he prayed for his friends: also the LORD gave Job twice as much as he had before. So the LORD blessed the latter end of Job more than his beginning." [Job 42:10,12]

YOU ARE GOING TO HAVE A WONDERFUL FUTURE!!!

Remember that ACTION keeps you positioned under the anointing so that you are as a new, sharp threshing instrument. Knowing that the enemy's KEY INTENTION is to STOP your action, you now have military intelligence as to his plans.

Your main focus NOW should be on developing a spirit of excellence in your actions. That's what *The University of Excellence* is about.

There are **SEVEN (7) things you need to cultivate a spirit of excellence:**

[1] VISION

Spend time with God. Pray and fast for:

- A fresh vision, and,
- A prophetic anointing.

[2] DETERMINATION

You need "bulldog" endurance and perseverance.

You can't be a "pansy" and you can't be a quitter. Be a warrior and remember: "If you don't quit, you will win!" (But if you quit, you can't win!)

[3] PRIORITIES

You need to put God's program FIRST in life. He will show you when you need to spend time for family, for recreation, and for fellowship. At times, He may have you spend LOTS of time on family, recreation, and fellowship. But don't try to replace God's Kingdom as your top priority. *"You seek first the kingdom of God, and all things will be added unto you."* [Matthew 6:33]

[4] ACCOUNTABILITY

Accountability will give you real liberty. You need to be accountable to:

- Messiah Jesus, the Great Shepherd; and,
- Others, who are ethical in your profession.

[5] REST

You need to rest one day a week. This is God's plan and is necessary for your overall long-term health and blessing. At times, He may lead you to take extended periods of rest. Always obey Him in these matters.

He knows what is best for you . . . and for those to whom you minister. You can't minister effectively if you're worn out or burnt out!

"For thus says the LORD God, the Holy One of Israel, In returning and rest you will be saved; in quietness and confidence will be your strength." [Isaiah 30:15]

Honoring and keeping the Sabbath will also enable you to appropriate the rewards of a spirit of EXCELLENCE: delight, dominion, and desires granted. [Isaiah 58:13-14]

[6] A HEART FOR GOD

The prophet Samuel said, "the LORD has sought him a man after his own heart," describing King David. [1 Samuel 13:14] After being anointed, and successful as a king and military leader . . . the champion of the people . . . King David sinned greatly. **Even in the midst of his sin, he had a heart toward God, which caused him to repent.** He paid dearly for his sin, but even in the midst of his sin, he loved God and was repentant.

In all his public official conduct he acted according to the Divine mind, and fulfilled the will of his Maker: thus was he **a man after God's own heart**. In reference to his private or personal moral conduct, the phrase is never used.

So what was his problem? Why did David sin? The answer is: **He didn't FEAR God**. He loved God, but He didn't fear Him at the time of his great sin! We need to be not only morally reverent towards God, but also to have a sense of alarm that will keep us from walking off the path of righteousness.

We need to think ahead of time about the consequences of our sin and transgression. Our Father in Heaven loves us too much to let us get away with such behavior. There is not much preaching on holiness anymore. We need to LOVE GOD and to FEAR GOD; then we will have a heart for God.

In David's rulership of the Kingdom – in his official conduct – he fulfilled the will of God; however, in his private life and personal conduct he failed miserably ... but then repented. This brings to light THREE very important things to consider:

■ Your actions can bring reproach on God, yourself, your family, your friends, your nation, and your cause.

■ Your actions can give your enemies occasion to slander you and also mock the God you are supposed to be serving.

■ Your actions can bring severe judgment upon you and your family.**In the heat of temptation you need to consider these things**. Are you willing to pay the price?

Do you LOVE God and your family enough to protect them from the results of your sin? Do you FEAR God enough to prohibit you from doing the thing(s) you are considering?

[7] INTEGRITY

Honesty and moral uprightness are the KEY INDICATORS of the God shaped life. **The deeper your character . . . the greater your impact!** Many things that we question in life – even small things – are a TEST of our integrity. God is constantly testing us to see if we can be entrusted with greater giftings, talents, skills, and responsibilities.

Integrity is a two edged sword. It is an instrument of blessing:

FOR OURSELVES

We must live with ourselves in all good conscience. *"For if our heart condemn us, God is greater than our heart, and knows all things. Beloved if our heart condemn us not, then we have confidence toward God."* [1 John 3:20-21] This assures us of answered prayer and provision. *"And whatsoever we ask, we receive of him, because we keep his commandments, and do those things that are pleasing in his sight."* [Verse 22]

FOR OTHERS

Our families, our friends, our associates and followers, our communities . . . our progeny . . . all are impacted by our integrity. The quality of our life is a direct antecedent of the same. The degree of EXCELLENCE of your life and ministry predetermines your future and many times, the future of those to whom you serve and love.

✦ ✦ ✦

Your integrity and faithfulness here on Planet Earth will also predetermine your future in the Millennial Kingdom with Messiah. Your position in the Kingdom and your assignment will be determined by the EXCELLENCE of your integrity and faithfulness here on earth.

LIVE A LIFE OF EXCELLENCE!

NOTICE

You just finished, *Action Keys for Success*.

Next, study the Companion Books in the
Success Series by Prince Handley:

    How to Do Great Works

    Success Cycles and Secrets

UNIVERSITY OF EXCELLENCE PRESS
Los Angeles ■ London ■ Tel Aviv

⊥

NOTE

We listen to our readers. Tell us what **new** subject matter you would like to see published. Email your ideas to: universityofexcellence@gmail.com.

OTHER BOOKS BY PRINCE HANDLEY

- Map of the End Times
- How to Do Great Works
- Flow Chart of Revelation
- Action Keys for Success
- Health and Healing Complete Guide to Wholeness
- Prophetic Calendar for Israel & the Nations: Thru 2023
- Healing Deliverance
- How to Receive God's Power with Gifts of the Spirit
- Healing for Mental and Physical Abuse
- Victory Over Opposition and Resistance
- Healing of Emotional Wounds
- How to Be Healed and Live in Divine Health
- Healing from Fear, Shame and Anger
- How to Receive Healing and Bring Healing to Others
- New Global Strategy: Enabling Missions
- The Art of Christian Warfare
- Success Cycles and Secrets
- New Testament Bible Studies (A Study Manual)

AVAILABLE AT AMAZON AND OTHER BOOK STORES
UNIVERSITY OF EXCELLENCE PRESS

www.ingramcontent.com/pod-product-compliance
Lightning Source LLC
Chambersburg PA
CBHW060648030426
42337CB00018B/3502